AF111867

This notebook belongs to:

_____

_____

Copyright © 2020
All rights reserved. No part of this publication may be reproduced,
distributed or transmitted in any form.

Idea: _____

_____
_____
_____
_____

Notes

Steps

_____
_____
_____
_____
_____
_____
_____
_____

Sketch / Doodle

Idea: _____

_____
_____
_____
_____

Notes

Steps

Sketch / Doodle

Idea: _____

_____
_____
_____
_____

Notes

Steps

Sketch / Doodle

Idea: _____

Notes

Steps

Sketch / Doodle

Idea: _____

_____
_____
_____
_____

Notes

Steps

Sketch / Doodle

Idea: _____

_____
_____
_____
_____

Notes

Steps

Sketch / Doodle

Idea: _____

_____
_____
_____
_____

Notes

Steps

Sketch / Doodle

Idea: _____

_____
_____
_____
_____

Notes

Steps

Sketch / Doodle

Idea: _____

_____
_____
_____

Notes

Steps

Sketch / Doodle

Idea: _____

_____
_____
_____
_____

Notes

Steps

Sketch / Doodle

Idea: _____

_____
_____
_____
_____

Notes

Steps

Sketch / Doodle

Idea: _____

_____
_____
_____
_____

Notes

Steps

_____
_____
_____
_____
_____
_____
_____

Sketch / Doodle

Idea: _____

_____
_____
_____
_____

Notes

Steps

_____
_____
_____
_____
_____
_____
_____
_____

Sketch / Doodle

Idea: _____
_____
_____
_____
_____

Notes

Steps

Idea: _____

_____
_____
_____
_____

Notes

Steps

Sketch / Doodle

Idea: _____

_____
_____
_____
_____

Notes

Steps

Sketch / Doodle

Idea: _____

_____
_____
_____
_____

Notes

Steps

Sketch / Doodle

Idea: _____

_____
_____
_____
_____

Notes

Steps

Sketch / Doodle

Idea: _____

_____
_____
_____
_____

Notes

Steps

Sketch / Doodle

Idea: _____

_____
_____
_____
_____

Notes

Steps

_____
_____
_____
_____
_____
_____
_____
_____

Sketch / Doodle

Idea: _____

_____
_____
_____
_____

Notes

Steps

Sketch / Doodle

Idea: _____

_____
_____
_____
_____

Notes

Steps

Sketch / Doodle

Idea: _____

_____
_____
_____
_____

Notes

Steps

Sketch / Doodle

Idea: _____
_____
_____
_____
_____

Notes

Steps

Sketch / Doodle

Idea: _____

_____
_____
_____
_____

Notes

Steps

_____
_____
_____
_____
_____
_____
_____
_____

Sketch / Doodle

Idea: _____

_____
_____
_____
_____

Notes

Steps

Sketch / Doodle

Idea: _____

_____
_____
_____
_____

Notes

Steps

Sketch / Doodle

Idea: _____

Notes

Steps

Sketch / Doodle

Idea: _____
_____
_____
_____
_____

Notes

Steps

_____
_____
_____
_____
_____
_____
_____
_____

Sketch / Doodle

Idea: _____

_____
_____
_____
_____

Notes

Steps

Sketch / Doodle

Idea: _____

_____
_____
_____
_____

Notes

Steps

Sketch / Doodle

Idea: _____

Notes

Steps

Sketch / Doodle

Idea: _____
_____
_____
_____
_____

Notes   Steps

Idea: _____

_____
_____
_____
_____

Notes

Steps

Sketch / Doodle

Idea: _____

_____
_____
_____
_____

Notes

Steps

Sketch / Doodle

Idea: _____

_____
_____
_____
_____

Notes

Steps

Sketch / Doodle

Idea: _____

_____
_____
_____
_____

Notes

Steps

Sketch / Doodle

Idea: _____

_____
_____
_____
_____

Notes

Steps

Sketch / Doodle

Idea: _____

_____
_____
_____
_____

Notes

Steps

Sketch / Doodle

Idea: _____

_____
_____
_____
_____

Notes

Steps

Sketch / Doodle

Idea: _____
_____
_____
_____
_____

Notes

Steps

Sketch / Doodle

Idea: _____

_____
_____
_____
_____

Notes

Steps

_____
_____
_____
_____
_____
_____
_____

Sketch / Doodle

Idea: _____
_____
_____
_____
_____

Notes   Steps

Idea: _____

_____
_____
_____
_____

Notes

Steps

Sketch / Doodle

Idea: _____

_____
_____
_____
_____

Notes

Steps

Sketch / Doodle

Idea: _____

_____
_____
_____

Notes

Steps

Sketch / Doodle

Idea: _____

_____
_____
_____
_____

Notes

Steps

Sketch / Doodle

Idea: _____

_____
_____
_____
_____

Notes

Steps

Sketch / Doodle

Idea: _____

_____
_____
_____
_____

Notes

Steps

Sketch / Doodle

Idea: _____

_____
_____
_____
_____

Notes

Steps

Sketch / Doodle

Idea: _____
_____
_____
_____
_____

Notes

Steps

Sketch / Doodle

Idea: _____
_____
_____
_____
_____

Notes   Steps
                       _____
                       _____
                       _____
                       _____
                       _____
                       _____
                       _____

Sketch / Doodle

Idea: _____

_____
_____
_____
_____

Notes

Steps

Sketch / Doodle

Idea: _____

Notes

Steps

Sketch / Doodle

Idea: _____
_____
_____
_____
_____

Notes

Steps

Sketch / Doodle

Idea: _____

_____
_____
_____
_____

Notes

Steps

_____
_____
_____
_____
_____
_____
_____
_____

Sketch / Doodle

Idea: _____

_____
_____
_____
_____

Notes

Steps

Sketch / Doodle

Idea: _____

_____
_____
_____
_____

Notes

Steps

Sketch / Doodle

Idea: _____

_____
_____
_____
_____

Notes

Steps

_____
_____
_____
_____
_____
_____
_____
_____

Sketch / Doodle

Idea: _____

_____
_____
_____
_____

Notes

Steps

_____
_____
_____
_____
_____
_____
_____
_____
_____

Sketch / Doodle

Idea: _____

_____
_____
_____
_____

Notes

Steps

Sketch / Doodle

Idea: _____
_____
_____
_____
_____

Notes

Steps

Sketch / Doodle

Idea: _____

_____
_____
_____
_____

Notes

Steps

_____
_____
_____
_____
_____
_____
_____

Sketch / Doodle

Idea: _____

_____
_____
_____
_____

Notes

Steps

Sketch / Doodle

Idea: _____

_____
_____
_____
_____

Notes

Steps

_____
_____
_____
_____
_____
_____
_____
_____
_____

Sketch / Doodle

Idea: _____

_____
_____
_____
_____

Notes

Steps

_____
_____
_____
_____
_____
_____
_____
_____
_____

Sketch / Doodle

Idea: _____

_____
_____
_____
_____

Notes

Steps

Sketch / Doodle

Idea: _____

_____
_____
_____
_____

Notes

Steps

Sketch / Doodle

Idea: _____

_____
_____
_____
_____

Notes

Steps

Sketch / Doodle

Idea: _____

_____
_____
_____
_____

Notes

Steps

Sketch / Doodle

Idea: _____

_____
_____
_____
_____

Notes

Steps

Sketch / Doodle

Idea: _____

_____
_____
_____
_____

Notes

Steps

Sketch / Doodle

Idea: _____

_____
_____
_____
_____

Notes

Steps

Sketch / Doodle

Idea: _____

_____
_____
_____
_____

Notes

Steps

Sketch / Doodle

Idea: _____

_____
_____
_____
_____

Notes

Steps

Sketch / Doodle

Idea: _____

Notes

Steps

Sketch / Doodle

Idea: _____

_____
_____
_____
_____

Notes

Steps

Sketch / Doodle

Idea: _____

_____
_____
_____
_____

Notes

Steps

_____
_____
_____
_____
_____
_____
_____
_____

Sketch / Doodle

Idea: _____

_____
_____
_____
_____

Notes

Steps

Sketch / Doodle

Idea: _____

_____
_____
_____
_____

Notes

Steps

Sketch / Doodle

Idea: _____

_____
_____
_____
_____

Notes

Steps

_____
_____
_____
_____
_____
_____
_____
_____

Sketch / Doodle

Idea: _____

_____
_____
_____
_____

Notes

Steps

_____
_____
_____
_____
_____
_____
_____

Sketch / Doodle

Idea: _____

_____
_____
_____
_____

Notes

Steps

Sketch / Doodle

Idea: _____
_____
_____
_____
_____

Notes

Steps

_____
_____
_____
_____
_____
_____
_____

Sketch / Doodle

Idea: _____

_____
_____
_____
_____

Notes

Steps

Sketch / Doodle

Idea: _____

_____
_____
_____
_____

Notes

Steps

Sketch / Doodle

Idea: _____

_____
_____
_____
_____

Notes

Steps

Sketch / Doodle

Idea: _____

_____
_____
_____
_____

Notes

Steps

Sketch / Doodle

Idea: _____

_____
_____
_____
_____

Notes

Steps

Sketch / Doodle

Idea: _____

_____
_____
_____
_____

Notes

Steps

Sketch / Doodle

Idea: _____

_____
_____
_____
_____

Notes

Steps

Sketch / Doodle

Idea: _____

_____
_____
_____
_____

Notes

Steps

Sketch / Doodle

Idea: _____

_____
_____
_____
_____

Notes

Steps

Sketch / Doodle

Idea: _____

_____
_____
_____
_____

Notes

Steps

Sketch / Doodle

Idea: _____

_____
_____
_____
_____

Notes

Steps

_____
_____
_____
_____
_____
_____
_____
_____

Sketch / Doodle

Idea: _____

Notes

Steps

Sketch / Doodle

Idea: _____

_____

_____

_____

_____

Notes

Steps

Sketch / Doodle

Idea: _____

_____
_____
_____
_____

Notes

Steps

Sketch / Doodle

Idea: _____
_____
_____
_____
_____

Notes

Steps

_____
_____
_____
_____
_____
_____
_____
_____
_____
_____

Sketch / Doodle

Idea: _____

_____

_____

_____

Notes

Steps

Sketch / Doodle

Idea: _____

_____
_____
_____
_____

Notes

Steps

Sketch / Doodle

Idea: _____

_____
_____
_____
_____

Notes

Steps

Sketch / Doodle

Idea: _____

_____
_____
_____
_____

Notes

Steps

Sketch / Doodle

Idea: _____

_____
_____
_____
_____

Notes

Steps

Sketch / Doodle

Idea: _____

_____
_____
_____
_____

Notes

Steps

Sketch / Doodle

Idea: _____

_____
_____
_____
_____

Notes

Steps

Sketch / Doodle

Idea: _____

_____
_____
_____
_____

Notes

Steps

Sketch / Doodle

Idea: _____

_____
_____
_____
_____

Notes

Steps

_____
_____
_____
_____
_____
_____
_____
_____

Sketch / Doodle

www.ingramcontent.com/pod-product-compliance
Lightning Source LLC
LaVergne TN
LVHW020134080526
838202LV00047B/3938